Cool

NANCY TUMINELLY

MEAT-FREE RECIPES

DELICIOUS & FUN FOODS WITHOUT MEAT

A Division of ABDO
ABDO
Publishing Company

visit us at www.abdopublishing.com

Published by ABDO Publishing Company, a division of ABDO, P.O. Box 398166, Minneapolis, Minnesota 55439. Copyright © 2013 by Abdo Consulting Group, Inc. International copyrights reserved in all countries. No part of this book may be reproduced in any form without written permission from the publisher. Checkerboard Library™ is a trademark and logo of ABDO Publishing Company.

Printed in the United States of America, North Mankato, Minnesota
102012
012013

♺ PRINTED ON RECYCLED PAPER

Design and Production: Mighty Media, Inc.
Series Editor: Liz Salzmann
Photo Credits: Aaron DeYoe, Shutterstock

The following manufacturers/names appearing in this book are trademarks: Pyrex®, Kitchen Aid®, Roundy's®, Del Monte®, Contadina™, Natural Value®, Steam of the Crop™, McCormick®, Spice Trend®, La Preferida®, Dunbars®, House of Tsang®, Ying's®, Enjoy Life®, East Wind™, Oster®, Osterizer®, Anchor®

Library of Congress Cataloging-in-Publication Data

Tuminelly, Nancy, 1952-
  Cool meat-free recipes : delicious & fun foods without meat / Nancy Tuminelly.
    pages cm. -- (Cool recipes for your health)
  Audience: 8-12
  Includes bibliographical references and index.
  ISBN 978-1-61783-582-7
1. Vegetarian cooking--Juvenile literature. I. Title.
  TX837.T86 2013
  641.5'636--dc23
                    2012023989

TO ADULT HELPERS

This is your chance to introduce newcomers to the fun of cooking! As children learn to cook, they develop new skills, gain confidence, and make some delicious food.

These recipes are designed to help children cook fun and healthy dishes. They may need more adult assistance for some recipes than others. Be there to offer help and guidance when needed, but encourage them to do as much as they can on their own. Also encourage them to be creative by using the variations listed or trying their own ideas. Building creativity into the cooking process encourages children to think like real chefs.

Before getting started, establish rules for using the kitchen, cooking tools, and ingredients. It is important for children to have adult supervision when using sharp tools, the oven, or the stove.

Most of all, be there to cheer on your new chefs. Put on your apron and stand by. Watch and learn. Taste their creations. Praise their efforts. Enjoy the culinary adventure!

CONTENTS

MEAT-FREE

GELATIN is made from the bones, skins, and tendons of animals. If you are on a vegetarian diet, avoid foods that contain gelatin.

People who don't eat meat are called vegetarians. Vegetarians don't eat red meat, **poultry**, or fish. Some vegetarians don't like the taste of meat. Others feel that not eating meat is important to their religion or **ethics**.

There are a lot of foods for people who don't eat meat. Try some of the vegetarian recipes in this book!

When shopping, look for fresh ingredients. Be sure to avoid things that might contain meat. Read the labels carefully.

Sometimes a recipe that includes meat will list vegetarian **options** for those ingredients. Or, be creative and make up your own **variations**. Being a chef is all about using your imagination.

SAFETY FIRST!

Some recipes call for activities or ingredients that require caution. If you see these symbols, ask an adult for help!

Hot - This recipe requires handling hot objects. Always use oven mitts when holding hot pans.

Sharp - You need to use a sharp knife or cutting tool for this recipe. Ask an adult to help out.

Nuts - This recipe includes nuts. People who are allergic to nuts should not eat it.

THE BASICS

ASK PERMISSION

Before you cook, ask **permission** to use the kitchen, cooking tools, and ingredients. If you'd like to do something yourself, say so! If you would like help, ask for it!

BE NEAT AND CLEAN

- Start with clean hands, clean tools, and a clean work surface.
- Wear comfortable clothing.
- Tie back long hair and roll up your sleeves so they stay out of the food.

NO GERMS ALLOWED!

Some raw ingredients may have bacteria in them that can make you sick. After you handle raw foods, wash your hands, tools, and work surfaces with soap and water. Keep everything clean!

READ THESE IMPORTANT TIPS BEFORE YOU START!

BE PREPARED

- Be organized. Knowing where everything is makes cooking easier!
- Read the directions all the way through before you start cooking.
- Set out all your ingredients before starting.

BE SMART, BE SAFE

- Never work alone in the kitchen.
- Ask an adult before using anything hot or sharp, such as a stove top, oven, knife, or **grater**.
- Turn pot handles toward the back of the stove to avoid accidentally knocking them over.

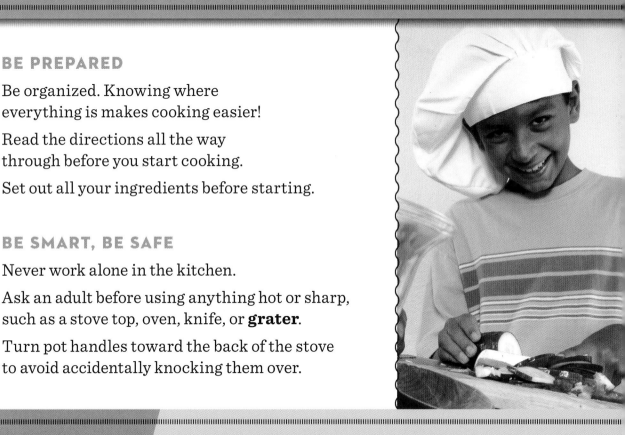

MEASURING

Many ingredients are measured by the cup, tablespoon, or teaspoon. Some ingredients are measured by weight in ounces or pounds. You can buy food by its weight too.

THE TOOL BOX

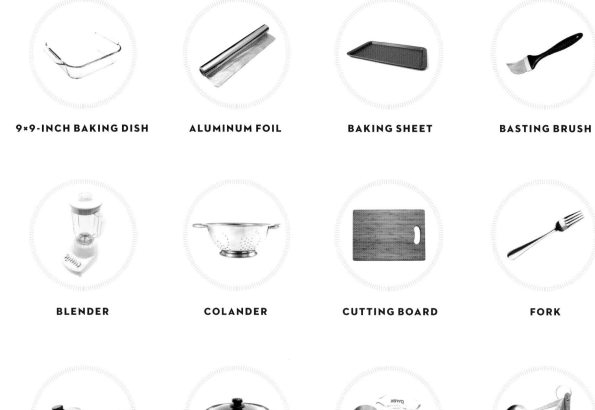

9×9-INCH BAKING DISH

ALUMINUM FOIL

BAKING SHEET

BASTING BRUSH

BLENDER

COLANDER

CUTTING BOARD

FORK

FRYING PAN

LARGE POT

MEASURING CUPS

MEASURING SPOONS

The tools you will need for the recipes in this book are listed below. When a recipe says to use a tool you don't recognize, turn back to these pages to see what it looks like.

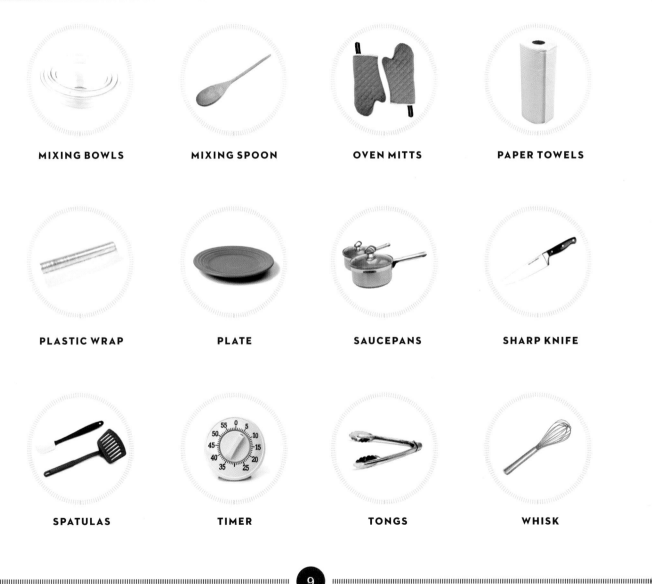

MIXING BOWLS

MIXING SPOON

OVEN MITTS

PAPER TOWELS

PLASTIC WRAP

PLATE

SAUCEPANS

SHARP KNIFE

SPATULAS

TIMER

TONGS

WHISK

COOL INGREDIENTS

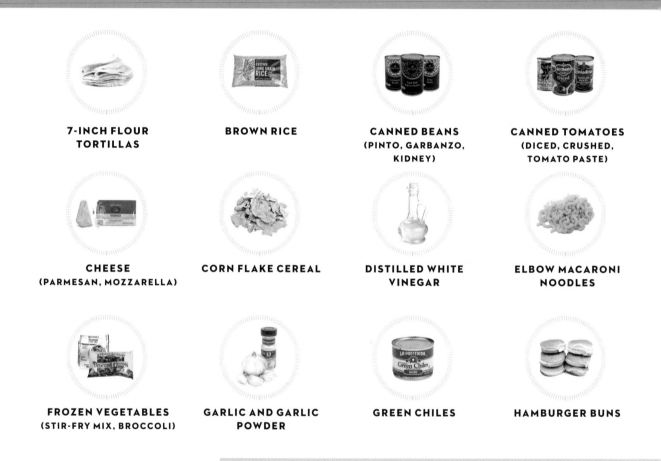

7-INCH FLOUR TORTILLAS

BROWN RICE

CANNED BEANS
(PINTO, GARBANZO, KIDNEY)

CANNED TOMATOES
(DICED, CRUSHED, TOMATO PASTE)

CHEESE
(PARMESAN, MOZZARELLA)

CORN FLAKE CEREAL

DISTILLED WHITE VINEGAR

ELBOW MACARONI NOODLES

FROZEN VEGETABLES
(STIR-FRY MIX, BROCCOLI)

GARLIC AND GARLIC POWDER

GREEN CHILES

HAMBURGER BUNS

FRESH VEGETABLES
carrots, celery, green bell pepper, green onions, onion, red bell pepper, and tomatoes

Many of these recipes call for basic ingredients such as black pepper, butter, cornstarch, eggs, non-stick cooking spray, olive oil, salt, and vegetable oil. Here are other ingredients needed for the recipes in this book.

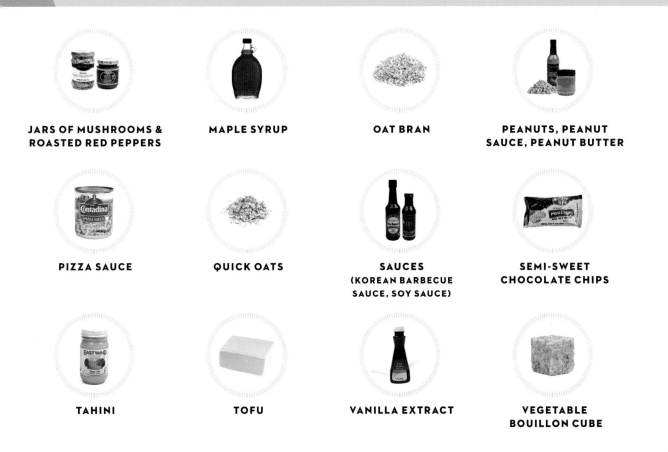

JARS OF MUSHROOMS & ROASTED RED PEPPERS

MAPLE SYRUP

OAT BRAN

PEANUTS, PEANUT SAUCE, PEANUT BUTTER

PIZZA SAUCE

QUICK OATS

SAUCES (KOREAN BARBECUE SAUCE, SOY SAUCE)

SEMI-SWEET CHOCOLATE CHIPS

TAHINI

TOFU

VANILLA EXTRACT

VEGETABLE BOUILLON CUBE

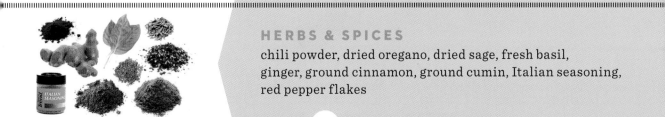

HERBS & SPICES

chili powder, dried oregano, dried sage, fresh basil, ginger, ground cinnamon, ground cumin, Italian seasoning, red pepper flakes

COOKING TERMS

BRUSH

Brush means to spread a liquid on something using a basting brush.

CHOP

Chop means to cut into small pieces.

DRAIN

Drain means to remove liquid using a strainer or colander.

GRATE

Grate means to shred something into small pieces using a **grater**.

MASH

Mash means to press down and smash food with a fork.

Always wash fruit and vegetables well. Rinse them under cold water.
Pat them dry with a **towel**. Then they won't slip when you cut them.

MINCE

Mince means to cut
or chop into very
small pieces.

ROLL

Roll means to wrap
something around
itself into a tube.

SLICE

Slice means to cut
food into pieces of the
same thickness.

STIR

Stir means to
mix ingredients
together,
usually with a
large spoon.

WHISK

Whisk means
to beat quickly
by hand with a
whisk or fork.

BREAKFAST BARS

makes 12 servings

INGREDIENTS

⅔ cup peanut butter

⅔ cup tahini

1½ cups maple syrup

4 cups corn flake cereal

2 cups quick oats

½ teaspoon ginger

½ teaspoon ground cinnamon

non-stick cooking spray

TOOLS

measuring cups & spoons

small saucepan

mixing spoon

9×9-inch baking dish

plastic wrap

sharp knife

timer

1   Put the peanut butter and tahini in a small saucepan. Stir over low heat.

2   Add the maple syrup and cook for 5 minutes. Stir often.

3   Remove the pan from the stove. Stir in the cereal, oats, ginger, and cinnamon.

4   Coat the baking dish with cooking spray. Spread the mixture evenly in the baking dish. Cover with plastic wrap. Put in the refrigerator for 1 hour.

5   Cut into squares. Eat one for breakfast or for a snack anytime!

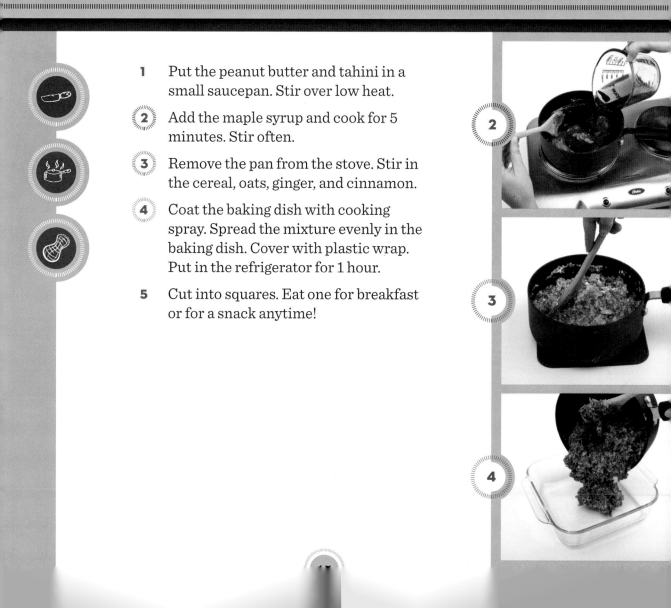

PIZZA PINWHEELS

makes 8 servings

INGREDIENTS

1 tablespoon butter

¾ cup onion, chopped

½ cup green bell pepper, chopped

½ teaspoon Italian seasoning

¼ teaspoon red pepper flakes

6 7-inch flour tortillas

8-ounce can pizza sauce

8-ounce package shredded mozzarella cheese

1 tablespoon vegetable oil

2 tablespoons grated parmesan cheese

TOOLS

baking sheet

aluminum foil

frying pan

measuring cups & spoons

large spoon

mixing spoon

sharp knife

cutting board

basting brush

oven mitts

timer

1   Preheat the oven to 400 degrees. Cover the baking sheet with aluminum foil.

2   Melt the butter in the frying pan over medium heat. Add the onion and green pepper. Cook about 8 minutes until tender. Stir in the Italian seasoning and red pepper flakes. Remove from heat.

3   Spread 1 tablespoon of pizza sauce over a tortilla. Leave ½ inch around the edge.

4   Put ¼ cup of the onion mixture on the sauce. Sprinkle shredded mozzarella on top.

5   Roll up the tortilla. Put it on the baking sheet.

6   Repeat steps 3 through 5 with the other tortillas. Brush the rolls with vegetable oil. Sprinkle the Parmesan cheese over them.

7   Bake for 8 minutes or until the cheese is melted. Remove the tortillas from the oven. Cut each tortilla into four pieces.

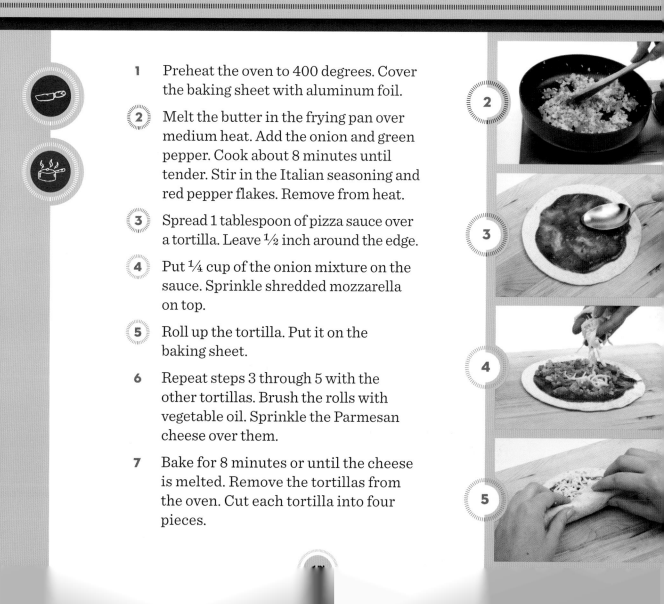

TOFU STIR-FRY

makes 8 servings

INGREDIENTS

vegetable oil

16-ounce package frozen stir-fry vegetables

½ teaspoon ginger, minced

salt and black pepper

2 eggs

1 cup cornstarch

14-ounce package firm tofu

¾ cup peanut sauce

¼ cup chopped peanuts

TOOLS

measuring cups & spoons

frying pan

mixing spoon

large mixing bowl

paper towels

sharp knife

cutting board

2 small mixing bowls

whisk

plate

timer

tongs

BECOME A FAN OF TOFU WITH THIS DELICIOUS MEAL!

1. Heat 1 teaspoon of oil in the frying pan over medium heat. Stir in the vegetables. Cook for about 5 minutes.

2. Add the ginger and salt and black pepper to taste. Put the vegetables in a large bowl and set aside.

3. Drain the water from the tofu. Pat the tofu dry with paper **towels**. Let it sit for 10 minutes. Cut the tofu into cubes.

4. Whisk the eggs in a small bowl. Put the cornstarch in a separate bowl.

5. Dip the tofu in the egg mixture. Then coat them with the cornstarch. Set them on a plate.

6. Heat ½ cup oil in the frying pan over medium heat. Add the tofu. Cook for 5 minutes. Turn the tofu with tongs to cook all sides until golden brown.

7. Stir in the peanut sauce and peanuts. Cook until the sauce thickens. Serve the tofu over the vegetables.

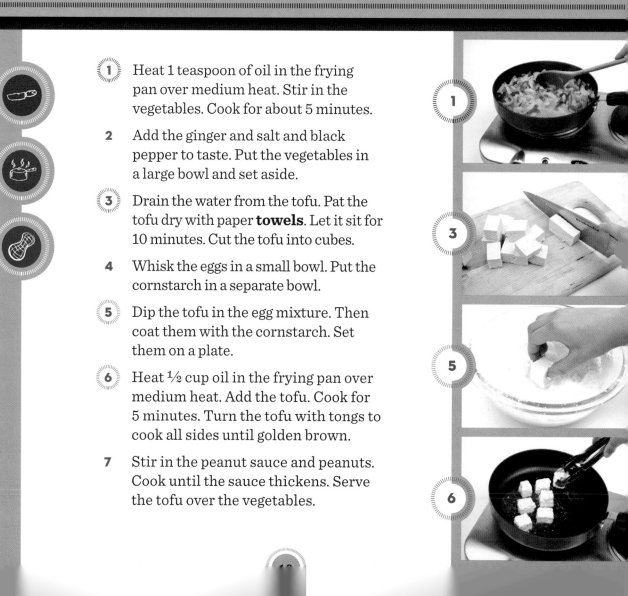

VEGGIE BURGER

makes 6 servings

INGREDIENTS

8-ounce can garbanzo beans, drained

4 fresh basil leaves, chopped

2 tablespoons oat bran

2 tablespoons quick oats

½ cup cooked brown rice

14-ounce package firm tofu

salt

2 tablespoons Korean barbecue sauce

¼ teaspoon black pepper

¼ teaspoon garlic powder

¼ teaspoon dried sage

1 tablespoon vegetable oil

6 hamburger buns

TOOLS

measuring cups & spoons

large mixing bowl

fork

mixing spoon

paper towels

frying pan

spatula

timer

1   Put the beans in a large mixing bowl. Mash them with a fork. Stir in the basil, oat bran, quick oats, and rice.

2   Drain the water from the tofu. Pat the tofu dry with paper **towels**. Sprinkle it with salt. Let the tofu sit for 10 minutes.

3   **Crumble** the tofu into small pieces. Put it in a bowl. Stir in the barbecue sauce.

4   Add the tofu to the bean mixture. Add the black pepper, garlic, sage, and ¼ teaspoon salt. Stir well.

5   Divide the mixture into 6 equal balls. Press each one into a flat patty.

6   Heat the oil in a frying pan over medium-high heat. Fry the patties for 5 minutes. Flip the patties over and fry for 5 more minutes.

7   Serve on buns with your favorite burger toppings.

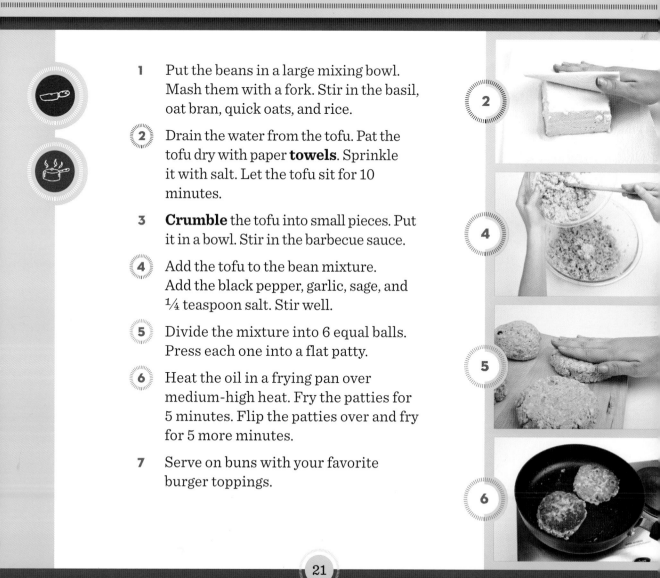

SLOPPY JOES

makes 8 servings

INGREDIENTS

1 tablespoon olive oil

½ cup onion, chopped

½ cup celery, chopped

½ cup carrots, chopped

½ cup green bell pepper, chopped

1 clove garlic, chopped

14.5-ounce can diced tomatoes

1½ tablespoons chili powder

1 tablespoon tomato paste

1 tablespoon distilled white vinegar

1 teaspoon black pepper

15-ounce can kidney beans, drained and rinsed

8 hamburger buns

TOOLS

measuring cups & spoons

sharp knife

cutting board

frying pan

mixing spoon

large spoon

timer

1. Heat the oil in a large frying pan over medium heat. Add the onion, celery, carrots, green pepper, and garlic. Cook about 5 to 10 minutes until the vegetables are tender.

2. Add the tomatoes, chili powder, tomato paste, vinegar, and black pepper. Stir well. Cover the pan. Reduce the heat to low. Cook for 10 minutes.

3. Stir in the kidney beans. Replace the cover and cook for 5 more minutes.

4. Put some of the bean mixture on each bun.

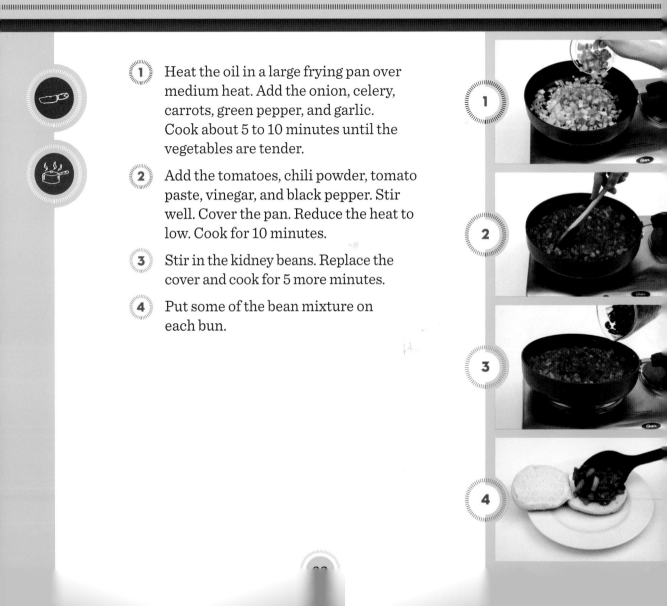

VEGGIE SIDE DISH

makes 8 servings

INGREDIENTS

2 tablespoons olive oil

3 large white onions, chopped

3 cloves garlic, chopped

¼ cup soy sauce

2 vegetable bouillon cubes

1 tomato, seeded and diced

7-ounce jar roasted red peppers, diced

4-ounce jar sliced mushrooms with juice

10-ounce package frozen chopped broccoli, thawed

3 green onions, chopped

1 cup cooked brown rice

salt and black pepper

TOOLS

measuring cups & spoons

large pot

mixing spoon

sharp knife

cutting board

timer

1. Heat the olive oil in a large pot over medium heat. Add the white onions and garlic. Cook for about 10 minutes until the onions are tender.

2. Add the soy sauce and bouillon cubes. Stir until the bouillon cubes **dissolve**.

3. Add the tomato, peppers, mushrooms, broccoli, green onions, and cooked rice. Stir well.

4. Continue cooking and stirring for about 7 minutes until the broccoli is soft. Add salt and black pepper to taste.

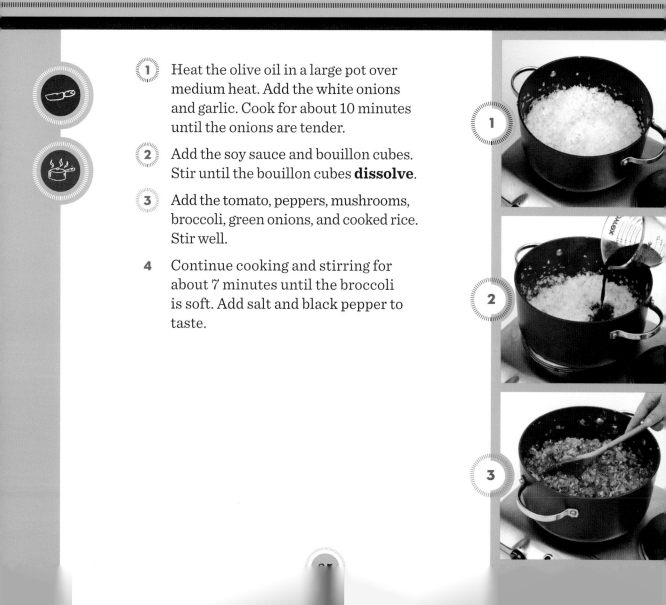

PUDDING SURPRISE

makes 4 servings

INGREDIENTS

16-ounce package soft tofu

¾ cup semi-sweet chocolate chips

3½ tablespoons maple syrup

1 teaspoon vanilla extract

TOOLS

blender

measuring cups & spoons

small saucepan

spatula

mixing spoon

1. Drain the tofu and break it into smaller pieces. Put the tofu in a blender. **Puree** it until it is very smooth. Hold the lid of the blender down while using it.

2. Put the chocolate chips in a small saucepan. Add the pureed tofu. Use a spatula to help scrape it out of the blender.

3. Heat the mixture over medium-low heat. Stir constantly until the chocolate chips have melted.

4. Add the maple syrup and vanilla extract. Stir well.

5. Remove from heat. Let the pudding cool to room temperature.

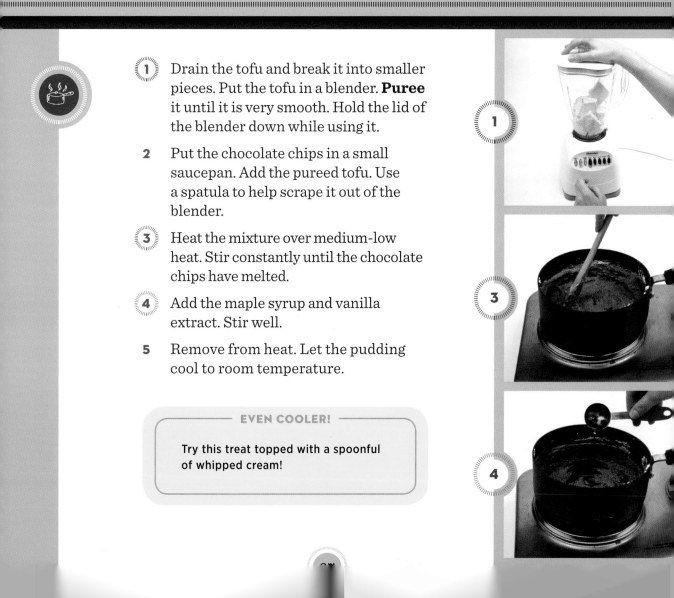

EVEN COOLER!

Try this treat topped with a spoonful of whipped cream!

CHA-CHA CHILI MAC

makes 6 servings

INGREDIENTS

2 tablespoons olive oil

1 large onion, finely chopped

1 medium green bell pepper, diced

1 medium red bell pepper, diced

4-ounce can mild diced green chiles

16-ounce can diced tomatoes

16-ounce can crushed tomatoes

2 16-ounce cans pinto beans, drained

1½ teaspoons chili powder

1 teaspoon ground cumin

1 teaspoon dried oregano

½ teaspoon ground cinnamon

10 ounces elbow macaroni noodles

TOOLS

measuring cups & spoons

sharp knife

cutting board

2 large pots

mixing spoon

colander

large mixing bowl

timer

28

1 Heat the oil in a large pot over medium heat. Add the onion and cook for 5 minutes. Stir in the green and red peppers. Cook for 4 minutes.

2 Add the remaining ingredients, except the noodles. Stir well.

3 Turn heat to low. When the mixture begins to bubble, cover the pan. Cook for 20 minutes. This is the chili.

4 Boil 4 cups of water in a separate large pot. Add the noodles. Follow the cooking directions on the package.

5 Drain the noodles. Put the noodles and chili in a large mixing bowl. Stir well.

EVEN COOLER!

To make this dish even more flavorful, sprinkle some grated cheese on top!

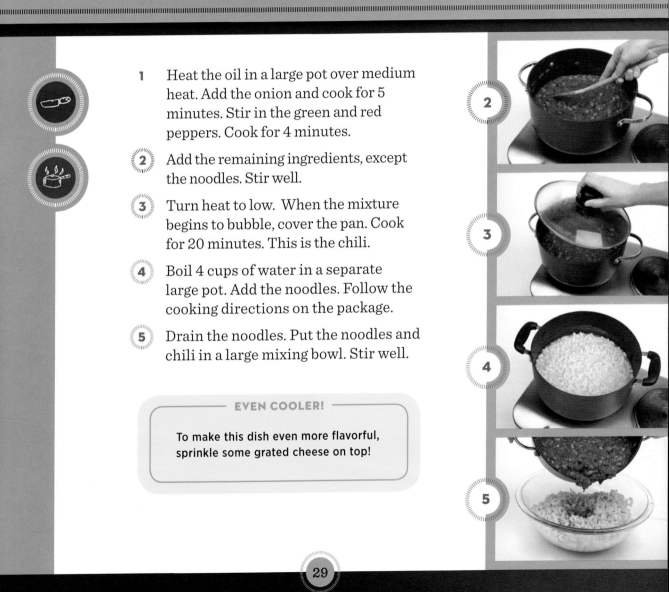

more about
MEAT-FREE LIFE

If you liked these dishes, look for other meat-free foods. If you want or need to avoid eating meat, you have a lot of **options**!

Many people use meat in the main course for a meal. Keep your kitchen stocked with healthy meat **alternatives**. Some great meat substitutes to try include soybeans, chickpeas, black beans, green beans, carrots, lentils, and tofu.

Now you're ready to start making your own meat-free recipes. It takes creativity and planning. Check out different cookbooks. Look through the lists of ingredients. You'll be surprised how many dishes don't need meat. Or you can come up with your own recipes or **variations**. The kitchen is calling!

It is important to eat a **variety** of fruits and vegetables. Then you won't miss out on important **nutrients**!

GLOSSARY

ALTERNATIVE - something you can choose instead.

CRUMBLE - to break into small pieces.

DISSOLVE - to become part of a liquid.

ETHICS - the rules of moral conduct followed by a person or group.

GRATER - a tool with rough-edged holes used to shred something into small pieces.

NUTRIENT - something that helps living things grow. Vitamins, minerals, and proteins are nutrients.

OPTION - something you can choose.

PERMISSION - when a person in charge says it's okay to do something.

POULTRY - birds, such as chickens or turkeys, raised for eggs or meat.

PUREE - to make very smooth and creamy using a blender.

TOWEL - a cloth or paper used for cleaning or drying.

VARIATION - a change in form, position, or condition.

VARIETY - a collection of different types of one thing. An assortment.

WEB SITES

To learn more about cooking for your health, visit ABDO Publishing Company on the Internet at www.abdopublishing.com. Web sites about creative ways for kids to cook healthy food are featured on our Book Links page. These links are routinely monitored and updated to provide the most current information available.

INDEX